The Best Bet

A play by Julia Donaldson

Illustrated by Charlie Alder

Characters

Tom

Emma

Mrs Smith

Callum

Ravi

Riya

Callum and Emma are at home with their mum.

Emma: I'm bored.

Callum: So am I.

Emma: Can we go to the park, Mum?

Mrs Smith: Have you finished all your homework?

Callum: Yes.

Mrs Smith: You too, Emma?

Emma: Yes.

Mrs Smith: Okay then. I'll come and fetch you at six.

Callum and Emma set off for the park.

Emma: I hope Ravi and Riya will be there.

Callum: I hope Tom will.

Emma: Yes he is, look! He's on that swing. Hi, Tom!

Tom: Hi, Emma! Hi, Callum! I bet you can't swing as high as this.

Callum: I bet I can.

Tom: Let's see then. You can be the judge, Emma.

The boys swing.

Emma: Tom's definitely higher.

Tom: Look, here come Ravi and Riya. I bet Ravi's going to stroke that cat over there.

Emma: No, I bet Riya strokes it.

Ravi: Hello, nice pussy-cat!

He strokes the cat.

Riya: Hi, you lot!

Emma: Okay Tom – you win.

Ravi: What do you mean?

Callum: Tom bet Emma that you'd stroke the cat, and you did.

Tom: I always win my bets!

Riya: I bet you don't! I bet you can't guess what we had for breakfast.

Tom: I bet you had cornflakes.

Riya: No we didn't!

Ravi: Yes we did, Riya. Don't tell fibs.

Riya: Okay Tom – you win.

Tom: See? I'm unbeatable!

Callum: Race you to that new slide.

Emma: It looks brilliant – it's really high.

Tom: How many steps do you think it's got? I bet thirty.

Ravi: I bet twenty.

Riya: I bet twenty-five.

Emma: I bet twenty-seven.

Callum: I bet forty.

Tom: I'll go up and count.

He climbs the slide.

Tom: Twenty-eight, twenty-nine, thirty! I was right!

Ravi: I bet he counted them before we got here.

Emma: Look, here comes Mum.

Callum: I bet Tom couldn't win a bet about her!

Tom: I bet I could.

Emma: What shall we bet?

Riya: I know! I'll whisper it to you.

Riya whispers her idea to the others.
Mum enters.

Mrs Smith: Callum! Emma! Tea's ready!

Callum: I think Tom would like a chat with you first.

Tom: Hello, Mrs Smith.

Mrs Smith: Hello, Tom.

Tom: I like your green shoes.

Mrs Smith: Thank you, Tom.

Tom: I bet you've got green toenails to match them.

Mrs Smith: I certainly haven't!

Tom: I bet you have!

Mrs Smith: Callum told me you like betting! But you're wrong this time.

Tom: I bet I'm not!

Mrs Smith: Look, I'll take my shoe off and show you. See – my toenails are red!

Tom: Oh yes. That's a shame. But I bet the ones on the other foot are green.

Mrs Smith: That's another bet you've lost, Tom. Look, I'll take this one off too. See — five more red toenails!

Ravi: Okay Tom – you win.

Mrs Smith: What do you mean?

Tom: They bet me I couldn't get you to take your shoes off!